GW00393341

21 insights

for 21st century creatives

BY MARK MCGUINNESS

21stCenturyCreative.fm

LATERAL ACTION BOOKS

21 INSIGHTS FOR 21ST CENTURY CREATIVES

First published by Lateral Action Books 2018
Paperback edition published by Lateral Action Books 2019

ISBN 978-1-9164714-1-2

Mark McGuinness is an award-winning poet, a coach for creative professionals, and the host of The 21st Century Creative podcast. He is the author of four books of career guidance for creative professionals, and also contributed to the 99U bestsellers *Manage Your Day-to-Day* and *Maximize Your Potential.*

"Mark McGuinness is a rare cat—part poet, part coach for creative professionals, part old-time, overeducated Brit who thinks deeply about stuff you and I have never heard of … a man who has lived the life and who has watched and worked intimately with hundreds of others who've done the same."
Steven Pressfield, bestselling author of *The War of Art*

"Of all the writers I know, I have learned the most about how to be a productive creative person from Mark. His tips are always realistic, accessible, and sticky."
Jocelyn K. Glei, Host of the Hurry Slowly podcast and Founding Editor, 99U

Also by Mark McGuinness

Resilience: Facing Down Rejection and Criticism on the Road to Success

Motivation for Creative People

Productivity for Creative People

To Issa, Kano, and Archie, who will soon know more about all this than I do

Contents

Introduction: 21 insights from 21 years of coaching creatives | 13

1 Everything is powered by love | 21
2 Reach for the stars | 25
3 Something old, something new | 31
4 Your creativity is your security | 37
5 Forget the career ladder—start creating assets | 43
6 Personal development is professional development (and vice versa) | 49
7 Your struggle is a clue to your superpower | 53
8 There are four types of work (and one matters more than the others) | 59
9 Desire beats discipline | 65
10 Your motivations are always mixed | 69
11 Play the game you want to play | 75
12 Pick two out of money, fame, and artistic reputation | 81
13 Find your medium, choose your media | 85
14 Stay small, go global | 91
15 Don't let the crappy part put you off | 97
16 Learn from the best in the world | 101
17 Be thankful for your Inner Critic | 107

18 Hustling is part of your job | 113
19 Stop trying to earn money—start creating value | 119
20 You can have all the excuses you want | 125
21 Courage may be the missing ingredient | 129

The 21st Century Creative podcast | 133
A free course for you | 135
More books by Mark McGuinness | 137
Coaching with Mark | 141

About Mark | 143
Thank you | 145

INTRODUCTION

21 INSIGHTS FROM 21 YEARS OF COACHING CREATIVES

introduction

21 insights from 21 years of coaching creatives

This is a book of insights to help you thrive as a creative professional amid the demands, distractions, and opportunities of the 21st century.

By "creative professional" I mean that you either earn a living from your creative work, or that you do it to a professional standard, even if you work in a non-commercial art form.

The insights cover a range of challenges and topics, including the psychology of creativity and success, the struggles of obscurity, the temptations of fame, the pros and cons of technology, the challenge of making a living, and how to get your most important work done.

The thread running through the book is the fundamental challenge faced by all creatives at this point in history:

How can you chart your course and make meaningful progress when you set out on an original path, where there is no conventional career ladder, no job security, and the usual rules don't apply?

In tackling this challenge, I have come up with answers you won't find in books of traditional career advice. And I didn't pluck them out of thin air—they emerged from two decades of conversations with hundreds of creative professionals like you, who were wrestling with these issues for real.

The book began as a blog post I published in December 2017: '21 Insights from 21 Years of Coaching Creative Professionals.' In many countries, 21 is the start of adulthood, so my 21st anniversary as a coach seemed like a good time to reflect on the previous two decades and share some of the key insights that had emerged from the thousands of one-to-one conversations I'd had with creative professionals over the years.

I got started as a coach by accident. Back in 1996, a year into my practice as a psychotherapist, I started to notice a pattern emerging. Mixed in with the people consulting me for anxiety, depression, addictions, work-related stress, relationship problems, and a host of other issues, was a different type of client. The actor with stage fright. The novelist with writer's block. The creative director dealing with the stresses of agency life. The entrepreneur on the rollercoaster of launching a business.

As a poet I found it easy to relate to these creative challenges, and there was a particular energy and intensity to these sessions. Clients walked away full of excitement, and came back to report big changes. They told me they had never experienced this kind of work before and encouraged me to keep at it.

I came to see that most of them didn't have a mental health problem in the clinical sense. As creative professionals, their work involved what Seth Godin would later call **emotional labor.** Because they put their heart and soul into their work, it made sense to work on their heart and soul.

So I decided to turn this into a new service for creative professionals, distinct from my therapy practice, and called it **creative coaching.**

Over the years I've worked with clients across the whole spectrum of the fine arts and creative industries—artists, writers, actors, musicians, designers, creative directors, film and TV scriptwriters, directors and producers, jewelers, dancers, sculptors, copywriters, art directors, TV and radio presenters, entrepreneurs, consultants, as well as other coaches and consultants.

Most of my clients have talents and technical skills I don't have. So I can't tell them what to do. But that's actually an advantage to me as a coach—because, free of industry jargon, assumptions about the "right" way to work, and their unseen personal limitations, I can ask them left-field questions driven by my own curiosity, to get to the heart of the matter.

Another benefit of working across art forms and industries is that I notice the kind of challenges that are common to most, if not all, creative careers:

Finding—and staying true to—your deepest sources of inspiration.

Carving out time to produce great work amid all the demands and distractions of everyday life.

Balancing creativity, money, and your professional ambitions.

Giving yourself a break from the relentless perfectionism of your Inner Critic.

Creating your own security in an uncertain world.

Charting your course and making meaningful progress in the absence of a conventional career ladder.

Selling your ideas to colleagues, clients, and investors.

Selling your artworks, products, and/or services to clients and customers.

Attracting an audience from scratch, or breaking into a tightly networked industry as an outsider.

Dealing with rejection, criticism, and plain unvarnished failure.

Deciding whether to approach publishers, record companies, or other middlemen, or to "go direct" to your audience.

Dealing with fear and anxiety—about your work, about your audience, about the critics, about failure, and even about success.

Having difficult conversations, where there's a lot at stake for everyone concerned.

Dealing with difficult people—clients, colleagues, business partners, critics, and others.

Getting your message across—in meetings, on the conference stage, on video, in media interviews, in books, in articles, and in proposals.

Dealing with the uncertainty of not knowing whether any given creative project—let alone your entire career—will turn out to be a success.

As you can imagine, I never have a dull week. When you combine the amazing projects my clients are engaged in with the ups and downs of navigating all these challenges, there is always plenty to talk about! It's exciting to be a small cog in the creative process of so many different types of work—from novels to feature films, conference speeches to fine art pieces. And it's a privilege to spend my time in the company of such inspiring professionals.

In the end, the coaching outgrew my therapy practice. After 19 years as a psychotherapist, I closed my practice to concentrate full time on coaching and my writing. I used to see most of my clients in person. I still see a few clients face-to-face, but most sessions are video calls with clients wherever they are in the world.

But there's a limit to the number of people I can help one-to-one. This book—and my podcast, The 21st Century Creative—is a way of going beyond the coaching conversation and helping more creative people to make the most of their talent and achieve their ambitions.

I have deliberately made the book short, with a brief chapter for each insight, so that you can keep it handy and consult it in the quiet moments of your day, or on those days when you need to dig deep for motivation.

So here are 21 insights from 21 years of helping creatives deal with the stresses and strains, joys and jubilations, of the creative life. I hope they help you create more and suffer less, whatever your creative path and wherever it leads you.

Mark McGuinness
Bristol, UK, August 2018

INSIGHT 1

EVERYTHING IS POWERED BY LOVE

1

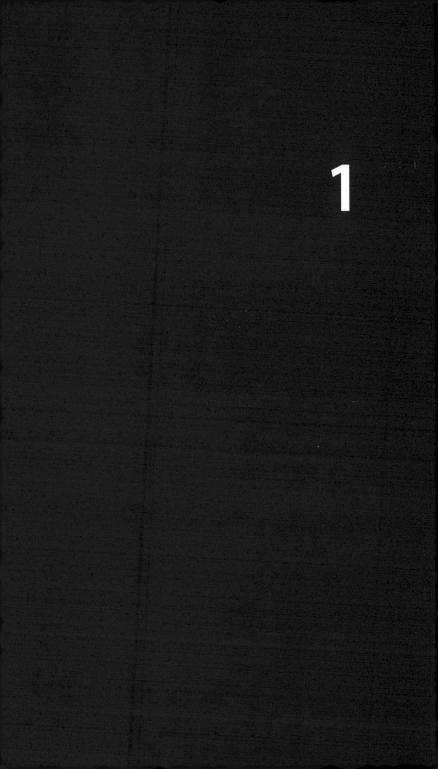

Everything is powered by love

If you don't love your work, you can forget it as a creative.
Psychologists talk about **intrinsic motivation** and tell us it is "proven to be highly correlated with creativity." But let's be honest: it's love.

You can probably remember the day you fell in love with your creative work: the butterflies in your stomach, your heart leaping, the sense of a whole new world opening up before you.

Maybe you saw another artist, creator, or performer doing something extraordinary and asked yourself: *Could I do that?*

Like all love affairs, it's probably been a rocky road with plenty of friction and suffering along the way. Maybe even a breakup or a trial separation. But you always come back, because this is the love of your working life.

With all the other pressures of work and personal life, it's easy to neglect this love, especially if you work in a non-commercial art, where the rewards are less obvious than the risks.

But if you neglect your true love, that neglect will poison everything else in your life.

So whether or not it supports you, whether or not it will make you famous, whether or not it will ever bring you worldly success, you need to find time and space for your creative work. When you do that, magical things start to happen.

And it's not just about the work. In the course of your career you will connect with many people—teachers, peers, partners, clients, customers, and others. If there is no love in these relationships, if they are driven by fear, competitiveness, and bitterness, is that really how you want to spend your days? And is that really how you will produce your best work?

So make sure you work with people you can respect and admire—and yes, even love.

Wake up every day to work on things you love, with people you love. What more could you ask of your career?

INSIGHT 2

REACH FOR THE STARS

2

Reach for the stars

We're not here for long. So why aim low?

It's so tempting to play it safe and aim for excellence in a familiar sphere. But by playing it safe you risk selling yourself short.

My best poems are usually written from a place of thinking *This is ridiculous but I can't resist trying it …*

Like translating Chaucer.

He's generally considered the second greatest poet in the English language, after Shakespeare. So who was I to start translating his masterpiece *Troilus and Criseyde* from medieval English into modern English verse?

But I couldn't resist … and I persisted, and was eventually awarded Third Prize in the 2016 Stephen Spender Prize, the UK's biggest competition for poetry translation.

I hear the same doubts from my clients when they talk about the challenges they set themselves: *This is ridiculous. Who am I to do that?*

Yet in spite of the doubts, and the obstacles in their way, they manage to create amazing things:

Fabrice Bourrelly is designing the future of virtual reality for the likes of Google, Thomas Heatherwick, and Epic Games.

Jane Armstrong recently emailed me to say she's won a major grant for her writing, from the National Endowment for the Arts in the US.

Josh Szeps took time out from his day job as a TV presenter to launch We The People Live, a podcast that has repeatedly topped the iTunes comedy charts.

Nick Dunin is on a mission to change the world by building a network of floatation tank centers.

Laurie Millotte launched Outshinery.com, an innovative business serving the wine industry, from her laptop while on a year-long round-the-world trip.

Ian Poitier expresses his passions for people, politics, and the arts by writing and directing television, film, and musical theater, and consulting on policy for national governments.

Steve Fudge coaches elite sprinters to win medals and break records.

Daniel Boettcher's company The Intrepid Wendell created a unique piece of jewelry, by persuading one of the finest goldsmiths in Japan to design a necklace for a two-times Olympic champion judoka.

Holger Nils Pohl uses visuals to facilitate workshops, meetings, and everyday communications to help companies such as Deloitte, Microsoft, and Roche solve their big strategic problems.

Emily Kimelman established herself as a best-selling thriller author while traveling across the US in an Airstream.

Javier Weyler has played drums with Stereophonics, Phil Manzanera, and Zak Starkey among other artists, in between making his own albums and creating soundtracks for movies, commercials, and documentaries.

Cornelius Frey quit his job as a successful consultant to found Opinary.com, a platform for sharing and tracking opinions utilised by *Bild*, *The Times*, NBC, *Frankfurter Allgemeine*, the *Guardian*, Toyota, and Deutsche Bank.

All of them, in the words of 'Roving Creative Director' Aileen Bennett, are "creating a job that doesn't exist," in order to make and do things that have never been done before.

When we look at what others have achieved, it's tempting to put them on a pedestal. We say they're lucky or naturally talented or well-connected—which is a great way to distract ourselves from our own dreams.

But I've seen up close what it takes to create something extraordinary. Mixed in with a lot of hard work, self-doubt, and determination, there is one quality we can all express if we choose: **daring.**

So reach for the stars.

(And be prepared for the shock of reaching them.)

INSIGHT 3

SOMETHING OLD, SOMETHING NEW

3

Something old, something new

You've probably heard that the 21st century is a time of incredible opportunity for creators. Changes in society and technology are opening up amazing new possibilities for creativity, collaboration, publishing, and distribution. According to the enthusiasts, there has never been a better time for making art and making money from it. If you can just find your thousand true fans, you can live the life of your dreams. You can travel the world as a creative entrepreneurial digital nomad ninja rock star.

And you can do all this because the means of production are in your pocket and on your desktop—not like the bad old days when they were in the factories of big bad capitalists, or the printing presses of publishers, or the studios of record labels or Hollywood. The gatekeepers have gone away and the creatives can come out to play.

On the other side are the doom-mongers telling us we're living in an age of trivia. Thanks to the internet and social media, we all have the attention spans of goldfish. We spend more time answering email and posting on Facebook than doing meaningful work. File-sharing, piracy, and the internet in general mean creators can no longer earn a living.

Musicians complain no one pays for music any more. Photographers complain everyone's using stock photographs, so no one pays for real photography. Writers and publishers complain that Amazon and ebooks are destroying publishing and killing literature. In short the 21st century is a terrible time to be a creator, even before we factor in climate change, terrorism, economic insecurity, political extremism, and all those robots coming to steal our jobs.

I'll admit I'm something of an enthusiast myself. You would be a little surprised if I were writing a book like this if I *didn't* think this was a time of opportunity and possibility for creatives. But there are definitely downsides to the brave new world. Here are two of them:

In the first scenario, you plow your lonely furrow in obscurity—maybe doing deep work and creating amazing things, but cut off from the world. You're not connected, not up to date with the latest trends in your field, and not getting your work out there.

In the second scenario, you enthusiastically embrace new ideas and technology, but you spend all your time on shiny new objects, learning the latest tools, trying out the trendiest new social media sites, frittering away your energy on trivia. Meanwhile you're neglecting your craft and avoiding the deep thinking that leads to truly great work. So however *busy* you may feel, you don't have a lot to show for it.

How, then, can you grasp the new opportunities without losing your creative soul? I suggest you take inspiration from the old wedding rhyme *something old, something new* and set yourself the modest ambition of becoming the most traditional and the most cutting-edge practitioner in your field.

Starting with the old, some aspects of creativity never change: the principles of storytelling, of human psychology, of balance and composition in a visual field, or the harmonic structures in music. Whatever your creative discipline, there are essential craft skills and an evolving tradition of great works. So there is always room to improve by working at these fundamentals.

Practice your craft. Do a deep dive into the history of your creative field. Study the old masters to learn the old techniques no one bothers with any more.

At the same time be open to new ideas, new skills, and new ways of doing things. Hang out with people in different fields. Take courses in technical or professional skills to help you achieve your ambitions and reap the rewards.

I often write poems that include modern or futuristic subject matter; but the verse form is likely to be from the Middle Ages. These days I'm in a minority of poets who use traditional forms—and at the same time I don't know many who are as comfortable as I am using digital technology and online media.

If I'd lived a hundred years ago I'd be writing everything in longhand. Twenty-five years ago I'd have been using a typewriter and typing the whole thing out again every time I wrote a new draft. Now I can edit on screen and print out a draft to review it. It's much easier to get a sense of the shape of a poem when it's laid out in pristine print than in my scruffy handwriting with lines crossed out and written over in my notebook.

I write in Scrivener, which is synced with my iPhone—so I have all my poems and book drafts in my pocket wherever I go. If I have a few minutes to kill or if inspiration strikes—on the subway, in a waiting room, or out for a walk in the woods—I can pull out my phone and start writing.

If you're a musician, you can record your music in high quality at home and play it back, add effects, and tweak it until you're satisfied. You don't have to go back very far to a time when this kind of technology was very expensive and reserved for genuine rock stars. Not much further back into history, and the technology didn't exist at all so the creative possibilities for musicians were a lot more constrained.

When I interviewed Patricia van den Akker for The 21st Century Creative podcast, she told me about designer-makers in remote parts of the UK who sell very niche products worldwide via the internet. Without this global reach their specialist craft traditions would probably be lost due to lack of demand—but the internet allows them to find enough enthusiastic customers for their micro-enterprises to thrive.

And so on. Whatever your creative field, the past opens up to you as a treasure trove, and the present offers new trends and technology to help you create your future works. Time to start exploring …

INSIGHT 4

YOUR CREATIVITY IS YOUR SECURITY

4

Your creativity is your security

When I started out, creativity was the risky option. I took it anyway and paid the price with years of struggle, compared to my friends who took the sensible jobs.

But the world has changed. These days the sensible jobs don't look nearly as secure as they did 21 years ago. Globalization, outsourcing, and automation, which have already gobbled up millions of blue-collar jobs, are now starting to gnaw at the white-collar positions.

No wonder Taylor Pearson recently proclaimed *The End of Jobs* in his book of that title.

The rise of the creative economy in recent decades means that creativity and innovation are essential sources of competitive advantage and economic prosperity. This has always been true in the arts and creative industries, but now it applies to every industry from farming to pharma, cars to carpets, finance to fine dining.

So far humans have been more creative than machines, so jobs involving "genuine creativity, such as being an artist, being a scientist, developing a new business strategy" are considered to be safest from the robots[1].

---

1 https://www.theguardian.com/us-news/2017/jun/26/jobs-future-automation-robots-skills-creative-health

Will the human advantage in creativity remain forever? I'd love to say "yes," but with AIs teaching themselves Go[2], writing black metal albums[3] and creating their own languages[4] to speak to each other, I'm not as sure as I would have been a few years ago. We're already starting to see automation encroach on such unlikely fields as acting, teaching, and psychotherapy[5]. But maybe as long as humans exist in their current form, we will value human creativity above the artificial kind.

Does this mean you'll be welcomed with open arms if you turn up at your local job center or recruitment office with your art portfolio under your arm? It probably won't be as straightforward as that. The most creative gigs typically don't go to the people who stand in line and wait. They go to the ones who create something amazing without asking permission or waiting for a commission. The ones who put themselves and their work out there, knocking on doors to make things happen. The ones whose track record is (eventually) so inspiring it starts to *attract* opportunities as if by magic.

It all starts with your attitude. The most successful and fulfilled creatives I've worked with embrace change and reinvent themselves in response to it. They don't sit around moaning about how the internet has disrupted their industry, or government funding for the arts has been slashed,

---

2 https://www.theguardian.com/science/2017/oct/18/its-able-to-create-knowledge-itself-google-unveils-ai-learns-all-on-its-own

3 https://www.digitaltrends.com/music/dadabots-ai-death-metal-album/amp

4 https://www.recode.net/2017/3/23/14962182/ai-learning-language-open-ai-research

5 https://www.theguardian.com/technology/2017/feb/09/robots-taking-white-collar-jobs

or publishers don't pay big advances any more. They ask themselves: *What can I do to take advantage of this? What new opportunities are there here for me?*

If you look around your creative scene, it won't be hard to find people complaining about the state of the industry. But take their whining with a pinch of salt. And seek out the dissenting voices—the ones talking about opportunity and possibility. Listen to them with an open mind to see what you can apply to your own career.

INSIGHT 5

FORGET THE CAREER LADDER—START CREATING ASSETS

5

Forget the career ladder —start creating assets

The traditional career ladder never worked for people like us, and as Insight 4 showed us, it's no longer even the safe option. So what's the alternative? How can you measure your success, and thrive creatively, professionally, and financially in this brave and uncertain new world?

By **creating assets** that will increase in value over time, bring you opportunities, and make it easier for you to create more, earn more, and achieve more.

In traditional economic terms, an asset is a piece of property that has value and can therefore help you meet debts and other financial commitments. Accountants like to distinguish between **tangible assets** (physical property, such as buildings and equipment) and **intangible assets** (virtual property, such as copyrights, trademarks, franchises, software, stocks, and bonds).

A crucial feature of an asset is that it is acquired or created *in the expectation of future reward.*

A developer buys property in the expectation of profiting from selling or renting it in future. An investor buys stocks in the expectation of future dividends. A company trademarks its name to protect its brand and the profits that flow from it. Publishers and studios acquire copyrights and trademarks in order to generate revenue from books and movies.

Now for the good news: **If you are a creator, you can create your own assets. Out of thin air. (Plus imagination and hard work.)**

I propose a special category of intangible assets called **creative assets.** These are the kind of assets you can create yourself and which will help you advance your career as a creative professional. Some of them generate money directly (e.g. royalty sales on your book or album), others will generate it indirectly (e.g. a stellar reputation attracting inquiries and opportunities).

Your portfolio of creative work

This is your signature asset, so it should always be your top priority. Keep creating work you are proud of, even if it has little or no direct financial value. You may be surprised how many ways it will add value to your career as well as to your life.

Your intellectual property

Besides the work itself, you own the copyright and other rights to the contents of your portfolio—assets you can license, sell, or otherwise exploit. You may register a **trademark in your brand** that adds value to your company, establishes trust with your customers, and opens up licensing opportunities.

Social assets

These include your brand, your network, your website, your mailing list, and social media profiles. All of these allow you to connect with people, to delight them, to serve them, and to get things done in outsize ways.

Artistic reputation

If you're an artist of any kind, you accrue reputation within your field through awards, prizes, reviews, and critiques, as well as your association with prestigious brands such as publishers, galleries, record labels, and performing companies. Your reputation may seem nebulous or even invisible to those outside your field, but for the ones "in the know," it is a very real asset that will attract valuable opportunities.

Business assets

If you're an entrepreneur, your business assets can include your range of products and services, your team and its intellectual and skills capital, and the company itself.

Systemic assets

These are intangible, but very powerful and valuable. Examples include a productivity system, a business process, or an innovative business model that generates a lot of value for your customers and your business.

Life is very different when you have a back catalogue of great work, a popular product range, an audience for your ideas, a network of great collaborators, and a string of lucrative licensing deals. You can get more done and earn more money, in less time, with less effort. So make it a priority to create the kind of assets that will help you achieve your artistic, professional, and financial goals.

Suppose you are Stephen King or Kate Bush or Neil Gaiman or Elon Musk. Do you wake up on a Monday morning filled with anxiety about how you will pay your bills? Do you wonder where your next project will come from? Do you struggle to persuade people to work with you? Obviously not. Because you have spent a lifetime doing great work and creating assets in the process—assets that act as magnets for income and opportunity.

No, we won't all reach the heights these creators have reached. But you don't need to be a global superstar to benefit from creating assets.

In my own case I've invested time in creating a popular blog, a podcast, and a series of books for creatives. These assets help attract the right kind of coaching clients to me—so I spend less time looking for clients than I used to, and more time serving my clients and writing. They have also enabled me to move from London to Bristol to be closer to my family and the countryside, while still growing my business.

To be clear, creative assets are *not* a substitute for the more traditional kind, like owning property or a stock portfolio. Don't bet the farm on your next novel being a bestseller! Although creative assets can complement other investments you make.

The critical point is that creating assets gives you a strategic focus for your creative career development—an alternative to the traditional career ladder. In the long term, creating and owning valuable assets will give you far more security than a job where you can be sacked or made redundant.

And I haven't even mentioned the most valuable asset of all …

INSIGHT 6

PERSONAL DEVELOPMENT IS PROFESSIONAL DEVELOPMENT (AND VICE VERSA)

6

Personal development is professional development (and vice versa)

As a creative professional, your most valuable asset—and potentially your biggest liability—is always yourself.

You can lose your money, your job, your business, even the copyright in your work—but you can always create more of all of these things, as long as you don't lose your creative mojo.

Working on yourself—building your skills, knowledge, mindset, resourcefulness, and resilience—is the smartest investment you can make in your creative career.

Every year I invest time, money, and energy on training, coaching, books, and other resources to learn new skills and improve the ones I already have. I'm a learnaholic, so I'd do it regardless of the payoff. But when I look back on the last 21 years, the time I spent learning looks like the most valuable time in my working life.

From this point of view, even a spiritual practice like meditation, or an exciting trip to an exotic destination, or learning a new language, or learning the hard way from rejection or failure helps you in your career because it can make you a richer, more creative, wiser, and more compassionate person.

Like the time I spent two weeks preparing a book proposal for a publisher—who didn't reply. My wife consoled me by saying, "Well at least you have another story to tell your clients!" And she was right—being a coach means I get to share my failures and disasters with clients and draw out the lessons for their benefit. (I still need to get the lesson for myself first!)

Developing yourself also works the other way round—every time you learn a new professional skill—public speaking, sales, marketing, negotiating, or financial literacy—you grow as a person. Every time you pursue a new goal in your career or business, it will challenge you and push you to draw on reserves of creativity, ingenuity, and courage that you didn't know you had.

I've done plenty of things for work that scared me witless. Things I'd never have dared to do if they hadn't been important for my career. Like public speaking. As a confirmed introvert, I had no natural inclination to stand up in front of an audience. But when I was offered a job as assistant trainer at a psychotherapy school, I realized I would have to get over my fear for the sake of my career. The first few times I stood up in front of the class, I was terrified. But I persisted, and with trial and error and some good coaching, I turned myself into a confident and engaging speaker, eventually speaking to audiences of several hundred people at prestigious conferences.

So as the years go by and you upgrade your phone, your computer, your car, and all the other important equipment in your life, don't forget to keep upgrading the most important equipment of all—yourself. Keep learning and seeking out new challenges. And next time an unexpected obstacle lands in your way, be thankful for the opportunity to rise to the occasion.

INSIGHT 7

YOUR STRUGGLE IS A CLUE TO YOUR SUPERPOWER

7

Your struggle is a clue to your superpower

For years it felt like my poetry and my career were fighting a duel to the death.

Time spent on poetry felt like an indulgence when I was struggling to earn a decent living. Time spent on my business felt like neglecting my true calling.

After a few threadbare years I had the opportunity to join a business coaching consultancy. I put on a suit, bought a briefcase, learned to use PowerPoint, and delivered training and coaching for big organizations. It worked very well up to a point—after the initial culture shock, I found I could help people from the shop floor to the boardroom. My partners and I did great work and we earned good money.

But as I got better at it and the challenge dipped, I found myself getting frustrated. I wanted to add a bit more spark, creativity, and whimsy into sessions.

One day, working with a group of corporate middle managers, I realized my analogies and flights of fancy weren't really connecting with them. I'd been struggling to fire them with curiosity about how their day-to-day management problems might look to aliens observing planet Earth or to time travelers from the distant past or future—and what creative solutions might emerge from these new perspectives.

I think we were all feeling a bit constricted by the prevailing corporate culture, which paid lip-service to creativity and empowerment but actually punished mistakes severely. On an impulse I asked them:

"Do I seem a little odd to you?"

They smiled kindly and nodded.

At that moment I realized that for this group, I needed to tone things down. But in the bigger picture, I saw that I was in the wrong place. I needed to take off the suit and spend more time working with my clients in the creative industries.

Yet even after I changed the focus of my client work, I neglected my poetry for long periods. It felt irresponsible to spend time writing poems during the working day, when I could be doing something to earn money.

Then one day my coach, Peleg Top, helped me see that the conflict was an illusion:

My coaching *supports* my poetry by providing time and other resources to practice my art.

And I wouldn't be the kind of coach I am without the poetry. It's one of the things that makes my kind of client want to work with me (and vice versa).

These days I spend most weekday mornings writing, with poetry taking its place alongside my other writing projects like my podcast and this book. The poems I'm currently working on are pinned up near my desk, so I keep looking at them and tweaking them in odd moments during the day. My first collection of poems is nearly complete.

Over and over I have seen the same pattern with my clients: your unique brand of struggle and suffering, the very thing that has dogged you and resisted you for years, may contain a clue to your superpower—the thing that marks you as unique and helps you achieve things you'd never have thought possible.

So next time this pattern appears in your life, ask yourself: *What if this were an important clue about my superpower? What lesson could it be trying to teach me?*

INSIGHT 8

THERE ARE FOUR TYPES OF WORK (AND ONE MATTERS MORE THAN THE OTHERS)

8

There are four types of work (and one matters more than the others)

On any given day there are four types of work you could be doing:

1. **Ongoing work:** things you have to do every day, every week, or every month to keep your world running smoothly—such as answering emails, attending meetings, or serving your clients.

2. **Events:** work related to one-off events or events that happen at intervals longer than a month—such as launching a book, playing a gig, running an event for a client, or speaking at a conference.

3. **Backlogs:** things you wish you'd done already and need to catch up on—an overflowing inbox, your end-of-year accounts, or a promise you made and haven't yet kept.

4. **Creating assets:** investing time in creating something that will generate ongoing value in the future—such as making art, writing a book, learning a skill, or building a mailing list.

Each type of work has its place, and its pros and cons …

Ongoing work

We all have ongoing work, and the chances are it includes a few things we'd rather not do. The challenge here is to avoid unnecessary drudgery and "busywork"—things that suck up time and creative energy without adding real value. Begin by eliminating as much as you can, so you're down to the essentials. Next, delegate as much as you can to other people or automate it using technology.

Finally, use systems and batch processing to do the rest as efficiently as possible. For example: if you answer your emails once or twice a day, you can burn through them without letting your inbox run your day. If you return all your phone calls one after the other, you'll be in the zone for conversations and you'll be more focused and engaging than if you make them one at a time, while you're in the middle of other things.

Events

Events are exciting and they are also mission-critical if you're a performing artist or an entrepreneur launching new products. In these cases events are part of the process of creating assets, so it's essential to do them and to do them well.

But for some of us events can be a distraction from our real mission. The adrenaline rush and urgent external demands can provide the perfect excuse to avoid the difficult challenge of building a portfolio of great work that will stand the test of time. If that sounds like you, then maybe it's time to reduce the number of events on your calendar and start attending to more creative matters.

Backlogs

Backlogs clog up our systems—and they usually have unpleasant consequences. So it's sometimes necessary to carve out time to clear a backlog. You feel great when you finally submit your tax return, or your expenses claim, or when your inbox is (relatively) empty and manageable, or when your studio is tidy and you can work without tripping over piles of clutter.

But clearing a backlog will only get you to zero. By clearing your desk or your inbox, you also clear your mind. Yet this is only valuable if you start using this mental bandwidth for more creative pursuits.

Creating assets

Insight 5 showed us that, by working on the self-started, mission-critical, original projects that will fulfill you as a creator and build your reputation over the long term, you create assets—the work you will look back on with satisfaction on your deathbed: "At least I did that." In Steve Jobs' phrase, this is the dent you make in the world.

It's also the riskiest kind of work in the short term. There is no guarantee a particular project won't fail. It's also the kind of work with the least external support and validation. Writing a book, starting a business, or learning a new art form is like being a marathon runner: everyone will be thrilled for you when you cross the finish line. But no one is there to cheer you on when you get up early on a cold winter morning and set out on a training run.

It feels good to clear a backlog, and great to take part in an exciting event. But over the long term, nothing will add more value to your creative career—artistically, financially, or emotionally—than creating assets. So make it a priority, not a pipe dream.

INSIGHT 9

DESIRE BEATS DISCIPLINE

9

Desire beats discipline

People sometimes say to me, "You must be so disciplined to sit down and write every day." But it's not discipline—it's *desire.*

To me, *discipline* sounds like an employee's word. It suggests that work is something you have to do, that is imposed from the outside and for someone else's benefit. Something you naturally resist and would rather avoid. If that's how you see your work—and if there is no one standing over you to make you do it—then of course you will need plenty of discipline to make yourself do it.

But is that really how you see your *creative* work? Surely it's something you *want* to do? In which case, why not just tap into your desire to do it?

This is what I do every morning. My writing routine isn't something I have to do or that I struggle to stick to. *It's how I get to do what I want to do.*

The rest of the day I have responsibilities and commitments—to my family, to my clients, to all the bills I have to pay. But those hours in the morning are precious to me. They are *my* time.

No, it's not always easy. I have to deal with distractions and interruptions just like every other creator. But desire is the fuel that keeps me going—desire to make a new poem or a new episode of my podcast or to get my ideas across to you in this book.

As long as you tell yourself you need discipline to do your creative work, you are putting an unnecessary barrier between yourself and your heart's desire.

Forget discipline. Focus on desire.

INSIGHT 10

YOUR MOTIVATIONS ARE ALWAYS MIXED

10

Your motivations are always mixed

I often hear creatives talk about "working for love" versus "working for money," as if the two were mutually exclusive. They aren't. But agonizing over this false dichotomy is a great way to hide from your next big challenge.

All successful creative professionals have mixed motivations for their work—there's an art to balancing them so that they *reinforce* each other instead of getting in each other's way.

Here are the four most important types of motivation for your creative career, from my book *Motivation for Creative People*:

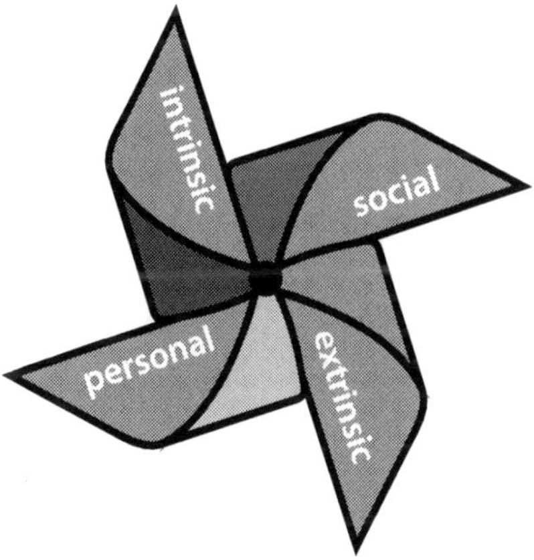

Intrinsic motivation—the joy of work

This is the "doing it for love" part. Psychologists confirm what we know in our hearts: intrinsic motivation is highly correlated with creativity. So if you are a creative, enjoying yourself is part of the job!

Extrinsic motivation—rewards for work

The "doing it for money" part. It's not just about money though—fame, artistic reputation, and opportunity are other big rewards on offer for creatives. While research shows that thinking about these things while trying to make art will kill your creativity, you need to factor them in at some stage if you want your career to be sustainable.

Personal motivation—your values

This is what drives you as an individual—things like knowledge, beauty, compassion, justice, pleasure, and power. Lose touch with your core values, and you experience all kinds of dissatisfactions, obstacles, and even mental and physical health symptoms. Staying true to yourself is a biological as well as a creative necessity.

Social motivation—the influence of other people

You may like to think of yourself as a unique and special individual, but your thoughts and actions are influenced by other people every day. Competition, collaboration, commitment, tradition, and rebellion are just some of the ways these influences play out. Any influence can be positive or negative—so think carefully about who you let into your life!

For your career to be successful and sustainable over the long haul, you need to *harness all four motivations.* If one or more are missing, sooner or later they will trip you up.

It's all very well following your heart and doing work you love, but the longer you struggle to earn a decent living or to achieve professional recognition, the more the (absence of) rewards will play on your mind, gnawing away at your enthusiasm for your work.

Sometimes you need to knuckle down and do what it takes to pay the bills, even if a particular job or freelance gig isn't particularly inspiring. But spend too long churning out work that gives you no pride or joy, and you start to feel like a sellout, getting further and further from your true calling.

Solitude can be great for focusing your mind, honing your craft, and cranking out great work. But if you're too much of a loner you cut yourself off, not just from companionship but also from the stimulation of other creative minds.

In an ideal world you'd have all four types of motivation in every project—it would be inspiring, lucrative, authentic to you, and recognized publicly in a big way. But if that seems out of reach (for now), don't despair—you may well be able to tick all four boxes by combining different roles and projects in the big picture of your career.

Maybe you have a relatively "uncreative" day job that gives you enough security and stability to create something eye-poppingly avant-garde in your spare time.

Or maybe you're a freelancer, taking on enough "money gigs" to keep the doors open and the lights on. You balance these out with more inspiring but less well-paid projects that feed your soul (and build your reputation among the discerning few).

Maybe you have two or more creative disciplines—all of which you enjoy but some of which are more commercially oriented than others.

What's the balance of different types of motivation in your creative life right now?

To find out, take a sheet of paper and divide it into four quadrants, one for each type of motivation.

Start with the **intrinsic motivation** quadrant and list all your current activities that bring you creative stimulation and fulfillment.

In the **extrinsic motivation** quadrant, list everything you do that brings you money or other extrinsic rewards, such as fame, artistic reputation, or new opportunities.

In the **personal motivation** quadrant, list everything you do that feels authentic and true to your deepest values.

In the **interpersonal motivation** quadrant, list everything that brings you energy and encouragement via contact with other people.

It's OK to put the same activity in more than one quadrant. In fact, that's a sign that it's a particularly meaningful and rewarding activity for you.

When you're finished, have a look at the sheet of paper. Which quadrants are fullest? Which quadrants look empty by comparison?

How can you start filling those empty quadrants to rebalance and strengthen your motivation for the journey ahead?

INSIGHT 11

PLAY THE GAME YOU WANT TO PLAY

11

Play the game you want to play

You've probably heard the good news: the game has changed for creatives in the 21st century. Instead of kowtowing to gatekeepers (editors, publishers, record labels, movie studios, and so on) creators are now free to publish and promote their work themselves.

If you listen to some of the keenest evangelists for this brave new world, only fools and fuddy-duddies would sign a book or record contract these days, or apply for representation by galleries or agents. Why not attract an audience online and sell direct to customers? Why jump through all those hoops and pay all those fees if you can do it all yourself, and pocket all the cash?

But what if you know for a fact that the people you want to reach still look to the gatekeepers as guarantors of quality?

The people who spend the most money on art tend to spend it with galleries, private collectors, and auction houses, rather than Etsy and artist websites. Readers of literary novels are often wary of self-published books. And believe it or not, there are still people who watch television—on actual televisions.

Or what if you're skeptical of the fact that self-publishing and going direct often seem to involve going via Amazon, Google, Facebook, or Apple?

Or what if you've always dreamed of being signed by your favorite record label or book publisher, or having your own TV show, or directing a Hollywood movie? Should you give up on your dream and turn to Amazon, Facebook, and YouTube instead?

Not if you ask me. I think you should play whatever game you want to play. Just make sure you're clear about *why* you're playing it.

If you really want to sign a book deal, or wait in line for a part in a movie, or hassle your agent to get you on TV, or network with the right people to get your art into the right galleries, then go for it.

As long as you're aware that you are paying for the opportunity—by relinquishing some control and maybe some money. If you're happy with the trade-off, then why not? (Just make sure you get a good lawyer to read that contract first.)

And if you want to do it yourself—by starting your own blog or podcast, or self-publishing your novel, or putting your album out on Bandcamp, then go for *that*.

If you're in this boat, you probably don't care what the *New York Times* critics or the people nibbling canapés at the private view think of your work. You probably relish the money and control more than their approval.

Just remember that no creator is an island—and don't complain if Amazon/Google/Facebook change the rules overnight and make a dent in your plans.

Or maybe you're a **hybrid creator**, looking to mix and match the best of both worlds, using the traditional channels when they work for you and the direct approach when they don't.

So maybe you work with a gallery when you want to exhibit your art in public to reach a certain type of buyer. But you also have a website where other buyers can find you, or where you sell prints or a different type of work than your gallery pieces.

Or maybe you work with a publisher to produce a book that requires lavish illustrations and beautiful printing and binding. But when it comes to a shorter collection of essays, you'd rather publish it quickly and easily yourself.

Or maybe you work on film and TV projects for studios and networks when they come along, but at the same time you have your own podcast or YouTube channel where you attract your own audience and create the kind of show that would never get aired on the big networks.

To me, the exciting thing about the 21st century isn't the fact that all the old media and gatekeepers and business models have vanished overnight, to be replaced by shiny new digital alternatives. It's the fact that **as creators we now have many more choices about how we make our work and get it out into the world.**

So play the game you want to play, whatever anyone else says. And remember they are all games, so don't forget to enjoy yourself while you're at it!

INSIGHT 12

PICK TWO OUT OF MONEY, FAME, AND ARTISTIC REPUTATION

12

Pick two out of money, fame, and artistic reputation

The previous insight showed us that we're spoiled for choice as 21st century creatives. We can either go the traditional route and work with publishers, galleries, record companies, movie studios, or TV networks. Or we can do it ourselves by blogging, podcasting, YouTubing, self-publishing, and selling from our own websites.

But you (probably) can't have everything. Especially when it comes to individual projects.

If you sign with a publisher, you give up a lot of control over the process—and a big chunk of the price of every copy.

If you self-publish, some people will look down their noses at you.

If you work with a gallery, you could find yourself contracted to an unscrupulous or incompetent owner.

If you sell your art from your website, you may not sell very much art from your website.

If you write avant-garde experimental poetry, you probably won't become world-famous.

If you do become world famous, people will queue up to say this proves you're not a real artist.

And so on …

As I said, it's up to you to choose what game you want to play. And any game you pick will give you a shot at one kind of reward and very likely exclude another.

Apart from the joy of creation itself, there are three main rewards on offer for creative work: money, fame, and artistic reputation.

Just to clarify the difference between the last two: fame is about **quantity**—how many people have heard your name? Whereas artistic reputation is about perceived **quality** within your creative field—how many influential critics, reviewers, and other creators consider your work to be of a high standard artistically?

You've probably noticed that it's perfectly possible for a creator to be held in high esteem as an artist while she's

broke and most people have never heard of her. On the other hand, someone may be world famous and earning pots of cash, producing work that is panned by the critics.

I assume that if you're reading this, nothing is more important to you than the sheer pleasure of creating. But I want you to look a little beyond that, to your professional ambitions, and ask yourself the question:

> *If I had to pick two out of money, fame, and artistic reputation, which would I pick?*

Of course there are exceptions—those annoying people like Charles Dickens or Pablo Picasso or Bob Dylan, who manage to become world-famous, filthy rich, and indisputably great artists, all at once. But even if you join them—and don't let me stop you—you'll enjoy the rewards all the more if you know which ones you care about the most.

INSIGHT 13

FIND YOUR MEDIUM, CHOOSE YOUR MEDIA

13

Find your medium, choose your media

One of your first tasks as a creative is to find your primary **medium—your means of expression.** This is composed of the raw materials and artistic forms you use in your work.

If you're a novelist, journalist, poet, or screenwriter, your medium is the written word. If you're a comedian or a conference speaker, your medium is the spoken word. Conversation is the medium of chat show hosts, psychotherapists, consultants, and podcasters. A photographer or painter's medium is made up of light and shadow, color and composition. Musicians play with rhythm, harmony, and melody. Movie directors work with actors, crew, and script.

Mastering your medium is the bedrock of your creative practice. It's how you do your best work, the work for which you will (hopefully) be remembered.

I say "find" your medium rather than choose it, because I don't think we have a choice in the matter. When you find your medium, it's more like discovery or recognition than a decision. When I was a boy, I used to draw and paint all the time, but as a teenager I fell in love with poetry and left my art behind. There was no choice to make.

To achieve mastery, it helps to have a teacher and a group of peers to spark off, compete with, and measure yourself against. It could be a class, a group of apprentices, the writers' room on a TV show, or the creative department in an agency. And whether you work alone or with others, there is no substitute for practice.

Mastering your medium is essential—but it's not enough. As well as a means of expression, you also need **media—a means of communication.**

Your media is how you share your work with the world. Without media, your medium won't amount to much more than a pile of manuscripts in your cupboard, or a hard drive full of brilliant work that no one sees.

In some cases, your medium and your media may be identical or very similar. If you're a columnist, then your articles are your medium, and their appearance in the newspaper constitutes your media. If you're a photographer, then it's a short step from taking a photo to publishing it on Instagram.

But in some cases a creative's medium and media can be different, but complementary. The non-fiction writer with a blog. The stand-up comedian with a YouTube channel. The artist with an email newsletter. The (ahem) poet with a podcast. And so on.

While I don't believe you choose your medium, I do think you can choose your media, and even change it. Choosing and building your own media platform can be a fun and rewarding challenge in its own right. And it may well evolve and change over time—as the media landscape changes, or you discover new and exciting ways to get your work out there.

Like your medium, your media will take time to master. You may well need a different teacher and group of peers to help you with this. Here are some other considerations:

It must not take too much time and creative energy away from your medium.

It must be enjoyable for you to produce—otherwise it won't be sustainable.

It must be attractive enough to your intended audience. It would be hard work promoting classical music on Snapchat. A 5,000-word essay may not get people into your cartoons (although it worked pretty well for Hugh MacLeod at GapingVoid.com, so don't rule anything out).

It should slot easily into your schedule. You could have a daily routine of sharing photos on Instagram or Tweeting from your phone. Or a weekly rhythm of recording video or audio, outside of your writing or painting or rehearsal time.

INSIGHT 14

STAY SMALL, GO GLOBAL

14

Stay small, go global

Once upon a time a small business was a local business. It was a small workshop where the owner and apprentices hammered away, weaving cloth, making tables, mending horseshoes, fixing bicycles, or servicing cars. It was the shop on the corner where we bought our newspapers and sweets, the bakery where we chatted with the lady behind the counter, the restaurant where the owner greeted us by name.

International businesses were big businesses, with fleets of cars, ships, and planes. The reception at head office proudly displayed clocks showing the times at the branch offices in London, New York, Paris, Hong Kong, and Tokyo.

For a while, ambitious small businesses went through a phase of pretending to be bigger than they were, with corporate-sounding brand names, and websites that said "we" even when there was only one person behind them.

One big exception was the creator who became an international star—the bestselling novelist, rock star, and TV or movie star. Like Archibald Leach, who was born just down the road from where I live in Bristol, England, and went to Hollywood to achieve worldwide fame as Cary Grant.

In 2005 Seth Godin wrote a seminal blog post called "Small is the new big."[1] He argued that the world was changing and people were coming to value the things *small* businesses

---

1 https://seths.blog/2005/06/small_is_the_ne/

were good at—such as personal service, flexibility, authenticity, and responsiveness. So small is the new big, but in Seth's words, "*only* when the person running the small thinks big."

About the same time I discovered Godin's work, I came across an interview with the advertising planner Russell Davies in *Campaign* magazine. He talked about launching a "global small business" with four partners, located in London, Amsterdam, Sydney, and New York. Every week, they held a weekly meeting inside World of Warcraft, where "we attack a castle or something, then chat about work." Which I thought was hilarious and inspiring in equal measure.

That was back in 2006, just after I'd started my first blog which I hoped would help me sell coaching and training to creative agencies in London. Once I started, however, I realized people were reading my blog from countries all over the world. One thing led to another, and I found myself delivering coaching sessions via Skype and receiving payments through PayPal—all without leaving the comfort of my home office. It certainly made a change from hiring an expensive office in central London, and commuting in and out for meetings.

Then I teamed up with two creative entrepreneurs in the US—Brian Clark and Tony Clark—to launch LateralAction.com. We spent two years as business partners without ever meeting face to face, growing a popular blog and selling e-learning courses to customers all over the world.

And it didn't stop at digital products. As my global audience and network grew, I was invited to speak at conferences in the US and Europe. I've also traveled to work with clients in North America, Europe, the Middle East, and the Caribbean.

In 2012 I joined the self-publishing revolution with several books that sold copies pretty well all over the world. And I have a publisher in Moscow—Mann, Ivanov, and Ferber—that publishes the Russian editions of my books.

Here in Bristol, this week alone I've worked with clients on three continents. Yesterday I worked with one client in Los Angeles and another in Tokyo. The day before it was Mexico and Paris. This afternoon it's New York and Canada. I've been doing this for years now, and it feels normal. I don't have the "London—Paris—New York—Tokyo" clocks in my office, but I do have an intuitive sense of what time it is in different parts of the world at different times of my day.

When I hit "publish" on a new blog post or podcast episode, it is sent out to thousands of people all over the globe. It's a magical feeling to log in to my Libsyn dashboard and look at the map showing where my podcast has been downloaded, with countries lighting up across North and South America, Europe, Africa, Asia, Australia, and Oceania.

I'm still a small business—it's just me, my Mac, a handful of carefully chosen clients, and a handful of carefully chosen collaborators. But I'm a *global* small business.

These days you don't need to be a big business or an A-lister to have a global audience or customer base. And you very likely can't rely on your local economy to support you. Keeping your enterprise small, you retain your freedom. Making it global can bring you opportunity and security.

INSIGHT 15

DON'T LET THE CRAPPY PART PUT YOU OFF

15

Don't let the crappy part put you off

The novelist Peter DeVries once quipped, "I love being a writer. What I can't stand is the paperwork."

Joking aside, whatever creative field you choose, I guarantee there will be a part you can't stand.

If you're a performer in the public eye, it may be the hours and minutes before you go on stage or on camera. Or the spite of gossip columnists or the intrusions into your personal life.

If you're an artist of any kind, it may be the endless hours of loneliness, procrastination, and self-doubt. Or the carping of critics, or the indifference of the public, or the infighting and backbiting of your peers.

If you're a commercial creative, it may be the demands and ingratitude of your boss, your clients, your team, or your business partner. Or on a bad day, all of them at once.

Whatever field you pick, there will always be a crappy part. And the crappy part will often have more to do with people and politics than the work itself.

If you're an amateur, you'll use the crappy part as an excuse to avoid showing up and challenging yourself. It will be the *perfect* excuse to avoid facing your fears and doing what it takes to make something great. But if you're a pro, you'll see through the excuse. So you will resolve to succeed *in spite of the crappy part*—either by ignoring it or by learning how to deal with it effectively.

This usually happens when you find work that you love so much you're prepared to put up with the crappy part.

But it also comes with the realization that whatever path you pick, *there will always be a crappy part*—there is no perfect creative path. At some point you're going to have to deal with the crappy part or give up altogether.

And you're never going to give up, are you?

INSIGHT 16

LEARN FROM THE BEST IN THE WORLD

16

Learn from the best in the world

If you want to do something amazing, the good news is, somebody somewhere has done something similar. So you can save yourself a lot of time, effort, and suffering by tracking them down and learning from their example.

A lot of creators think doing something original means avoiding any kind of influence, but actually the reverse is true: you usually start by watching someone else, wishing you could be like them, and following their example. Except that you never make an exact copy—you take something of what they do and add your own twist to it, so it turns into something that looks and feels all your own.

When Steven Sondheim was a boy, he was friends with a neighbor named James Hammerstein. James's father was Oscar Hammerstein of Rodgers and Hammerstein fame. Sondheim had written a musical that had been performed at school and received very well. Everyone was praising his precocious talent.

But Sondheim wasn't satisfied. Knowing Oscar Hammerstein's achievements, he made a very brave request. He asked Hammerstein to critique his musical as if he had never heard of its author.

Hammerstein said it was the worst thing he had ever seen. "But if you want to know *why* it's terrible, I'll tell you."

And he spent a whole day going through Sondheim's musical, pulling it apart and showing the young composer how to make it better.

Sondheim later said, "In that afternoon I learned more about songwriting and the musical theater than most people learn in a lifetime."

These days Sondheim is the revered master. Obviously he would never have achieved what he's done without talent and hard work. But he was also brave enough and humble enough to ask for help from an experienced teacher.

In my own career I've been blessed with world-class mentors—John Eaton in psychotherapy, Mimi Khalvati in poetry, Brian Clark in marketing, Steven Pressfield in writing about the creative life, Peleg Top, Rich Litvin, and Steve Chandler in coaching, and Kristin Linklater in speaking poetry.

I will never surpass any of them in their own field—but I don't have to. I'm on my own path, and the point of mentorship is to take what you can from your teacher and apply it in your own way.

When you have multiple mentors, a lot of the value you create comes from your unique blend of their different influences. I know several other students of each of my mentors who are further along their particular path than I am. But I don't know anyone who has quite the same mix of mentors as I do.

I say I've been blessed with these mentors, but it wasn't entirely down to luck—in every case I either reached out to the person directly, or I did something that put me on their radar and led to a connection.

John, Mimi, and Kristin were teaching classes, so I signed up as a student. John also became my psychotherapy supervisor and later my business partner.

Brian was teaching an online course so I joined it. Based on what I learned, I sent a joint venture proposal to him and his partner, Tony Clark. It felt like a long shot—but they accepted right away and we launched the Lateral Action website together.

Writing the Lateral Action blog was how I got on Steven Pressfield's radar—one of his team saw the blog and sent it to Steve. Soon afterwards I was interviewing him for the blog, and we've been in touch ever since.

My blogging and book writing also brought me invitations to speak at conferences in the US. I met Peleg when we were both speaking at the HOW Design conference in Boston, and our friendship and working relationship developed from there. It was Peleg who introduced me to Rich and Steve.

So if you're really committed to being the best you can be, take time to reflect on these questions:

Who is the best in the world at what I do?

How did they get to be that good? Have they written or spoken about this process, or been interviewed about it?

What can I learn from their example?

And if you *really* want to take things to the next level, ask yourself:

Do they take students or give public talks?

How can I get on their radar and into their circle of influence?

INSIGHT 17

BE THANKFUL FOR YOUR INNER CRITIC

17

Be thankful for your Inner Critic

Just about every creative I've ever coached has had a very sharp and active Inner Critic.

And you know what? That's a good thing.

If you find yourself resisting this idea, maybe because you know what it's like to suffer with an over-active Inner Critic, then pause for a moment and consider all the mediocre work you've encountered in your field. You know, the half-baked stuff that looks like it was put together in five minutes. The stuff devoid of taste, originality, authenticity, and/or basic craft skills.

This is the kind of work produced by people with an *under*-developed Inner Critic, or even no Inner Critic at all. Your Inner Critic is your own Critical Faculty, which is essential to producing great work. It's the part of you that can appraise a piece of work and tell you what works and what doesn't—and why. The part of you that knows you can do better and can point you in the direction of how.

And yes, it has a downside. Left to its own devices, the Inner Critic can run amok, giving you a constant negative critical commentary, not just on your work, but on you as a person. You're not a real artist, it tells you. *You'll never amount to anything. What makes you think you can achieve anything worthwhile when you churn out crap like this?* Ad nauseam.

The Inner Critic can be hard to live with, yet a finely honed Critical Faculty is one of the things that separates a successful professional from the legions of amateurs. So how can you get the benefits without the downside?

Think of a highly trained sushi chef. One of his prized possessions is a razor-sharp knife. The sharpness is essential for the delicacy and precision of his work. So the knife needs handling with care and attention.

But what does the chef do at the end of the day? *He puts it away. Safely out of reach. Where it won't injure anyone.* Then he leaves work and spends time with his friends and family, enjoying the fruits of his labors. Next morning he comes back refreshed and sharp for a new day's work—just like his knife.

What he *doesn't* do is stick the knife in the back pocket of his jeans, or sling it in his rucksack, or twirl it casually in his hands as he saunters home from work, or use it to point or gesture while he's having a beer with friends or dinner with his family. He knows what damage the knife can do, so he leaves it behind with his work.

Treat your Critical Faculty like that sushi knife.

Keep it sharp and finely honed—by keeping up with the latest work in your field, as well as learning from the Old Masters. Engage your peers in discussion about the merits of the work you discover. Read critiques and reviews of other creators' work and think critically about what you read. Get expert feedback on your own work. Learn to assess your work with a coolly objective (not over-critical!) eye. Write articles or give talks about your creative heroes, articulating why you think their work is great.

The more you consciously exercise your Critical Faculty, the more you take ownership of it—so the less likely it is to manifest as a low-grade, nagging voice at the back of your mind.

Be particularly watchful for the fatal shift from critiquing a piece of work to criticizing yourself. Whether or not you're a "real artist" or a deluded amateur isn't for you to decide. What is up to you, every day, is to get better at appraising your work and making it better.

And at the end of each day, *put your knife away.* Let go of the urge to critique, and don't take it seriously. Give yourself the benefit of the doubt until tomorrow morning, when you can start afresh.

INSIGHT 18

HUSTLING IS PART OF YOUR JOB

18

Hustling is part of your job

If I had a bitcoin for every creative who has told me *I'm really good at my work, so why am I struggling?* I could fund a manned mission to Mars.

If you're a maker or performer who says, *I just need someone to deal with the business side of things while I get on with my work*, or a creative service provider who says *Just put me in a room with a client and I'll get on with the job*, you are kidding yourself.

Because dealing with the business side of things is your job. And getting in the room with the client is your job.

Hustling—in other words, engaging with people and making things happen—is your job.

Yes, you can get great people to help you. But handing over "the business side of things" lock, stock, and barrel to someone else is asking for trouble. There are plenty of stories of artists and creatives who did this—and got into trouble because they didn't read the small print, and didn't understand the implications of the decisions they were delegating to the so-called professionals.

Until you accept that hustling is part of your job, you will suffer and struggle. The sooner you accept it and the better you get at it, the sooner you will taste success.

Yes, I know it's hard and you would rather be doing other things. Maybe you don't feel you are a born hustler. Tell me about it! As an introverted British poet, I felt I couldn't be less suited to hustling. But I made it my business to learn—and to find ways of doing it that are authentic for me. If I can do it, so can you.

Maybe you're thinking, OK, but I don't know how to do it. If that's the case, then I wonder whether "knowing how to do it" is the real problem.

As the coach Steve Chandler is fond of pointing out, if you really want to know how to do something, there are lots of ways you can learn:

If you Google it, you'll find lots of articles with advice on how to do it.

If you search on Amazon, you'll find plenty of books full of advice.

If you search on iTunes or YouTube, you'll find podcasts and videos explaining how to do it.

If you look for courses and teachers, you'll find plenty of those too.

You probably do this already, when you really want to learn something—whether it's a language or a sport or a new creative technique.

And for all those things, you probably accept that there won't be a cookie-cutter solution or an obvious "right way" to do it. Different teachers will have different advice, and you'll have to go through a period of trial and error as you learn through experience what works best for you.

It's the same with the business side of your career—it will take time and trial and error. What works for other people may need to be adapted to fit your own situation. But if you really play full out, and throw yourself into the learning process, you can get there.

The biggest step is often the first step—accepting that this is part of your job and committing to learning it for real.

INSIGHT 19

STOP TRYING TO EARN MONEY—START CREATING VALUE

19

Stop trying to earn money —start creating value

You may not always be aware of it, but you create your own reality every moment of the day—through the words you speak, the words you write, and even the words you *think* to yourself.

One of the things we're really good at as human beings is telling ourselves and each other stories about the way the world is—where it came from, what it all means, and what our place is in the grand scheme of things.

Take money, for instance.

You're probably familiar with the story that we all "have to earn money" to survive. It's a story that fits the facts pretty well. If you're living in a society that uses money to allocate resources, then it will be awkward, to say the least, if you find yourself short of cash at the end of the month.

But watch out for that little word "earn." Its meaning seems obvious enough, but if you think about it, it could really mean just about anything. Look at all the different things people do to "earn money" and you'll see what I mean.

And the connotations of "earning" money can be very insidious and disempowering. When you think about "earning" something, you probably think of putting in a lot of hard work and effort, even suffering. You might also think about whether you "deserve" something, whether it's fair for you to receive it.

So as long as you tell yourself you "have to earn money," you are living in a world of hard work, drudgery, and suffering. Money is tied to effort. So it feels somehow wrong to earn it without putting in a lot of effort.

On the one hand you can feel guilty if you find yourself earning a lot of money without working really hard and suffering a lot. Or even while *enjoying* yourself.

And on the other hand you can easily—and mistakenly—assume that simply working harder will bring you more money. I've fallen into that trap several times, by working really hard inside a system that wasn't working. The harder I pushed the faster my wheels would spin—but I wasn't gaining any traction or earning any real money.

But if you forget about earning money and focus on **creating value,** you enter a different world. A world where your income is not tied to the effort you put in, but to the value you create for others—whether that value is practical, financial, emotional, or experiential.

In this world a single painting can be sold for millions of dollars. A single song or book or movie can touch millions of hearts—and sell millions of copies.

One of the wonderful things about being a creative is that *there is virtually no limit to the value you can create for others,* and therefore potentially no limit to the money you can generate. Just look at the money created by the most successful painters, designers, actors, musicians, authors, architects, and entrepreneurs.

So forget about "earning money"—it feels too much like hard work.

Instead, focus on creating value—*also known as what you can do for others*—and start to ask yourself different kinds of questions:

What's the most valuable part of my work?

Who values it the most?

In what way is it valuable to them? Artistically? Emotionally? Practically? Or in some other way?

What could I create that these people would value even more?

Are there more people like them, who would value my work the way they do? How can I reach them?

Write these questions down and pin them up above your desk. Look at them every day for a week and write down all the answers that come to mind. Notice what a difference this makes—to your mood and energy, as well as to the quality of your ideas.

INSIGHT 20

YOU CAN HAVE ALL THE EXCUSES YOU WANT

20

You can have all the excuses you want

My life changed the day I realized I could have all the excuses I wanted—and I didn't want any of them.

I was struggling to drum up business, caught in a seemingly endless cycle of rejection and disappointment, and running out of money and self-belief.

After yet another dispiriting phone conversation with a prospect who had turned into a time-waster, I saw that I had every excuse to give up. I looked around at my rented room, with piles of sales books and tapes stacked next to poetry books, and realized this could be my last day of self-employment if I wanted it to be. If my business was a dog, I thought, the kindest thing would be to put it down.

I could tell my business partners I'd done my best, that it was simply too difficult, taking too long—and they would totally understand. They'd be sympathetic and tell me how much they respected me for trying.

I could count on plenty more sympathy—from my girlfriend, my friends, and my family. No one would blame me for giving up.

I saw that I had plenty of excuses at hand—but at that moment I knew that *I didn't want the excuses. I wanted to succeed.* And I was going to do whatever it took to make it happen. Which I (eventually) did.

If you ever get to the point of giving up—on a creative project, on a business, even a career path—remember you can always find an excuse to give up. There's no shame in changing your mind.

Just make sure giving up is what you *really* want to do.

INSIGHT 21

COURAGE MAY BE THE MISSING INGREDIENT

21

Courage may be the missing ingredient

If you're feeling frustrated and wondering why you're (still) struggling, ask yourself:

> *When was the last time my heart was in my mouth as I started to write? Or as I opened my mouth to speak? Or I stepped out on stage? Or I hit the "publish" or "send" button?*

If it has been a while since you challenged yourself so much that you created a situation calling for bravery, then maybe it's time to rediscover your courage.

Because maybe the problem isn't the quality of your work. Or the value of your services. Or your branding. Or your website. Or your network. Or any of that other stuff you've been trying to fix.

Maybe you've simply been playing small—out of fear.

One of the things I find myself repeating over and over to clients is: *The bigger the dream, the bigger the fear.*

When you dream a big dream, it will enchant you and sparkle enticingly. New vistas will open up before you. Its promise will beckon you forward.

But once the initial rush of excitement has passed, you start to think of all the things that could go horribly wrong. That's the fear kicking in.

Fear is actually a sign that you're on the right path—dreaming and daring big. Welcome it—because if you don't experience much fear, it's not much of a dream.

So why not set out on a **fear safari** and start hunting for the fear in your everyday life—in your studio, in conversations, in front of an audience, when you're one-on-one, when you're all alone?

And when you find some fear, big or small, congratulate yourself. Because you've just discovered your chance to step up and be braver, right this instant.

THE 21ST CENTURY CREATIVE PODCAST

Many of the insights from this book originally appeared on my podcast **The 21st Century Creative**—the show that helps you succeed as a creative professional amid the demands, distractions, and opportunities of the 21st century.

Each episode features more insights from me, plus in-depth interviews with outstanding creators—including artists, writers, performers, commercial creatives, directors, producers, and entrepreneurs. I also feature experts on topics of particular relevance to creatives, such as creativity, productivity, technology, personal development, leadership, marketing, and creative entrepreneurship.

Guests include Steven Pressfield, Tina Roth Eisenberg, Scott Belsky, Jocelyn K. Glei, Todd Henry, Joanna Penn, Kristin Linklater, Josh Szeps, and Michael Bungay Stanier. Plus more amazing creatives you've probably never heard of who are creating weird and wonderful things in the nooks and crannies of the creative industries.

In each interview I focus on the essential factors that are common to any creative career—things like inspiration, mindset, courage, and resilience in the face of adversity. I ask my guests about their deepest motivations, and the highs and lows of their particular path to success.

Whatever your own creative discipline, I hope you'll find something to relate to and something to inspire you in every episode.

You can find all the episodes of the show on iTunes and at:

www.21stCenturyCreative.fm

A FREE COURSE FOR YOU

THE 21ST CENTURY CREATIVE FOUNDATION COURSE

Over 10,000 people have taken my free 26-week creative career training, The 21st Century Creative Foundation Course.

The course covers the whole range of skills you need to succeed as a 21st Century Creative, including:

- creative thinking
- productivity for creatives
- growing your network
- promoting your work
- selling without selling your soul
- managing money
- dealing with rejection and criticism
- making the most of your intellectual property
- creative presentation skills

21st Century Creative students are also the first to know when I release a new book (usually at a discount).

You can get the whole course for free at:

LateralAction.com/FreeCourse

MORE BOOKS BY MARK MCGUINNESS

PRODUCTIVITY FOR CREATIVE PEOPLE

How to Get Creative Work Done in an 'Always On' World.

Productivity for Creative People is a collection of insights, tips, and techniques to help you create time for your most important work—while managing your other commitments.

All the solutions I share in the book have been tried and tested in my own work and with my coaching clients.

Read *Productivity for Creative People* to learn how to create extraordinary work without (necessarily) disappearing to a cabin in the woods, or even giving up your smartphone.

"Many creative people are busier than ever, but rarely get around to the work that truly matters. Mark McGuinness offers solid and practical advice for busy creative people who want to make their mark on the world."
Todd Henry, author of *The Accidental Creative*

LateralAction.com/Productivity

MOTIVATION FOR CREATIVE PEOPLE

How to Stay Creative While Gaining Money, Fame, and Reputation

A practical guide to figuring out your different motivations and how they affect your creativity and career.

This book tackles the "creativity vs money" issue head on, and shows that they are *not* necessarily incompatible—but they do require careful handling if money and other types of reward are not to kill your creativity.

"*Motivation for Creative People will encourage you to reflect sincerely on the factors that underpin your artistic achievements, ultimately giving you a 'clarity of mission' that will take your creativity to new heights.*"
Jocelyn K. Glei, host of the Hurry Slowly podcast and Founding Editor, 99U

LateralAction.com/Motivation

RESILIENCE

Facing Down Rejection and Criticism on the Road to Success

Rejection and criticism are a fact of life for creative professionals. Resilience explains why it's almost impossible *not* to take rejection and criticism of your creative work personally—and what to do about this.

It also shows you how to have more constructive conversations about feedback—with your boss, your colleagues, and your clients. Most of all, it will show you how to keep going in the face of rejection and criticism, and how to use them to strengthen your resolve and make your work better.

"Achilles' mother dipped him, as an infant, into the River Styx to make him invulnerable. Mark McGuinness does the same for you and me with Resilience: Facing Down Rejection and Criticism on the Road to Success. Read this book and you will be bulletproof!"
Steven Pressfield, bestselling author of *The War of Art*

LateralAction.com/Resilience

“

Mark’s unique skill as a coach is being able to empathize as a creative professional, but also challenge as an ambitious entrepreneur.”

Joanna Penn

New York Times & *USA Today* bestselling author

COACHING WITH MARK

I coach creative professionals who want to achieve great things with their lives.

They are drawn from the entire spectrum of the creative industries: fine artists, performers and entertainers, commercial creatives, and creative entrepreneurs.

They live all over the world—the magic of the internet means I can coach them wherever they live.

I help them with their creativity, their productivity, their communication and presentation skills, their writing, their branding and marketing, their sales, their networking, their money, their strategy, their business model, and their collaboration and leadership skills.

But most of all I help them show up as their most creative, courageous, and resilient selves—at their desks, in the studio, on stage, with their own clients, or in front of the cameras. And behind the scenes, I help them handle the pressure, make the big decisions, and have the difficult conversations that are unavoidable on the road to success.

I do this because I know what it's like to be the odd one out, the one with the crazy vision, the one who feels compelled to do things his or her way.

I do it because I know how lonely it can feel on those days when you have to make a big decision, or deal with a big unexpected problem, or hold true to your vision when the people around you don't get what you're trying to do, or why.

And I do it because I know what it's like to have someone in my life who really understands me and my vision, who will support and encourage me to be my best self—and who won't accept anything less than my best.

I want to be that person for them. Maybe I could be that person for you …

Does this sound like you?

This is the kind of person who will get the most out of working with me:

Most importantly: You are engaged in meaningful creative work, and you want to achieve something extraordinary in the course of your career.

You are a creative professional with at least five years' experience in your field.

You have a goal big enough to give you the shivers—of excitement tinged with fear—each time you think about it.

A goal that keeps you up at night.

A goal that will transform your work as a creative—and change your life.

You want to work with someone who "gets" you as a creative, and who won't steer you towards the conventional path.

You are prepared to work on yourself—by letting go of the beliefs and behaviors that have been holding you back, and by experimenting with new ways of doing things.

You aren't looking for cookie-cutter solutions—you're past the stage of wanting someone to tell you what to do.

You're ready to play full out and take bold action in pursuit of your dreams.

If that sounds like you, then let's talk.

You can learn more about my coaching, read client testimonials, and apply for a coaching place, here:

LateralAction.com/Coaching

ABOUT MARK MCGUINNESS

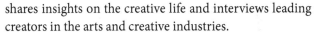

Mark is an award-winning poet who has been coaching creative professionals since 1996.

Based in the UK, he coaches clients all over the world, and consults for creative agencies and studios.

Mark is the host of **The 21st Century Creative podcast,** where he shares insights on the creative life and interviews leading creators in the arts and creative industries.

He is the author of *Productivity for Creative People*, *Motivation for Creative People*, and *Resilience: Facing Down Rejection and Criticism on the Road to Success.*

He also contributed to two international bestsellers from 99U, *Manage Your Day-to-Day* and *Maximize Your Potential.*

Mark's work has been featured in *Creative Review*, the *Wall Street Journal*, *Vogue US*, and on the Discovery Health Channel.

THANK YOU!

To all the coaching clients I have worked with over the past 21+ years—it's been a privilege and an inspiration to share your journey.

To John Eaton, Roy Johnson, Peleg Top, Rich Litvin, and Steve Chandler for helping me to become a better coach.

To David Colin Carr, my editor, for helping me to express my thoughts more clearly, and to Sarah Ridley for her meticulous proofreading.

To Irene Hoffman, for designing the cover and interior pages of this book, and the identity of The 21st Century Creative Podcast.

To Javier Weyler and his team at Breaking Waves Agency, for the music and sound production of The 21st Century Creative Podcast.

To Mum and Dad, for never trying to persuade me to get a proper job.

To Mami, Kano, and Issa for making it all worthwhile.

Printed in Great Britain
by Amazon

34236506R00090